UNDER PRESSURE

Thanks to Alexandra Muse and Pamela Auchincloss for taking the initiative to organize and tour this exhibition, and for believing that Two Palms Press was making interesting things to look at and think about. And a special thanks to all the artists who have allowed me the privilege of working with them.
—DL

The exhibition tour was organized by Alexandra Muse, Seattle and Pamela Auchincloss/Arts Management, New York.

Lyman Allyn Museum of Art at Connecticut College, New London, CT
February 2 – April 1, 2001

The Schick Art Gallery, Skidmore College, Saratoga Springs, NY
July 12 – September 16, 2001

Meadows Museum, Southern Methodist University, Dallas, TX
October 22 – December 8, 2001

University Gallery, University of Massachusetts at Amherst, MA
February 2 – March 15, 2002

Kent State University Art Gallery, Kent, OH
September 4 – September 28, 2002

625 Williams Street
New London, CT 06320

Photography credits: Peter Moscato (Terry Winters, Sol LeWitt, Jessica Stockholder); Shandor Hassan (Pedro Barbeito); James Dee (Chuck Close, SELF-PORTRAIT 1); Jean Vong (Chuck Close, SELF-PORTRAIT 2; Tara Donovan; Carroll Dunham; David Row); David Lasry (studio shots); Jeff Goldberg/Esto (cover image).

Library of Congress Card Number 00–111588
ISBN 0–295–98119–9

Designed by white.room productions, New York
Printed in Hong Kong at C & C Offset Printing, Ltd.

Catalog distributed by University of Washington Press
P.O. Box 50096
Seattle, WA 98145
206-543-4050

Cover:
Print Workshop, Two Palms Press

UNDER PRESSURE

Lyman Allyn Museum of Art at Connecticut College
University of Washington Press, Seattle & London

PRINTS FROM **TWO PALMS PRESS**

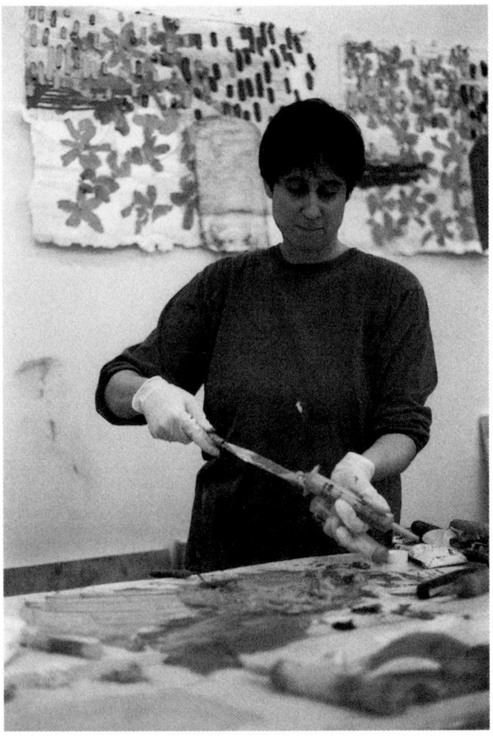

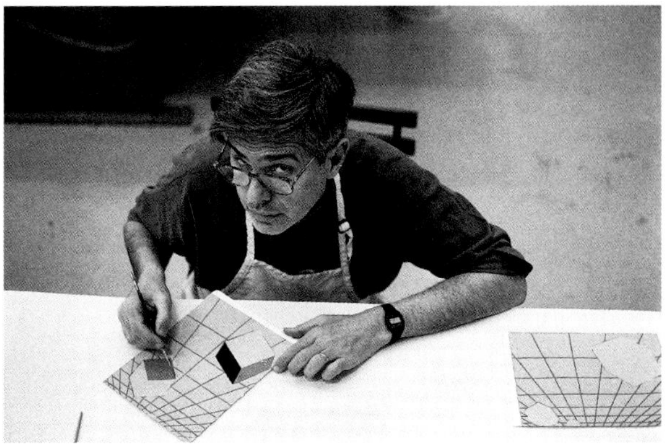

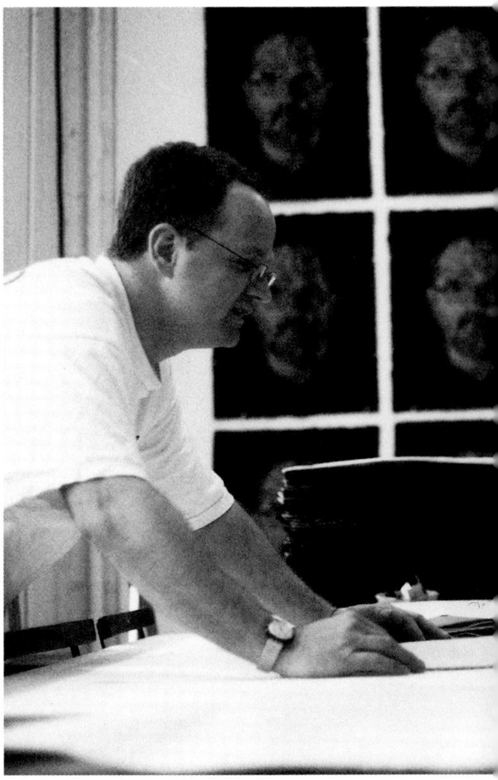

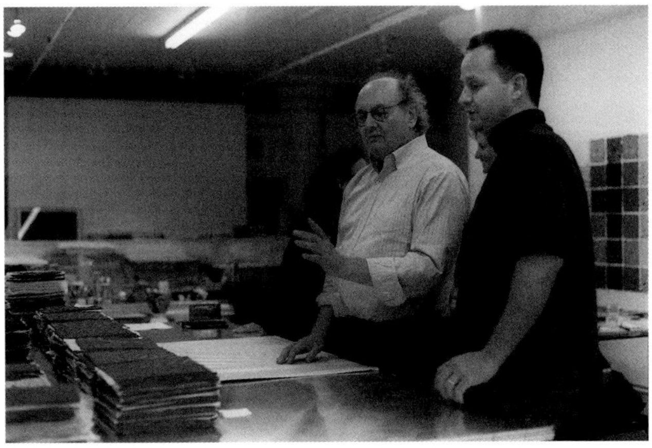

From top left to bottom right:

Jessica Stockholder, Mel Bochner, Tara Donovan, David Lasry with Chuck Close, Lasry with Sol LeWitt, Carroll Dunham, Lasry with David Row.

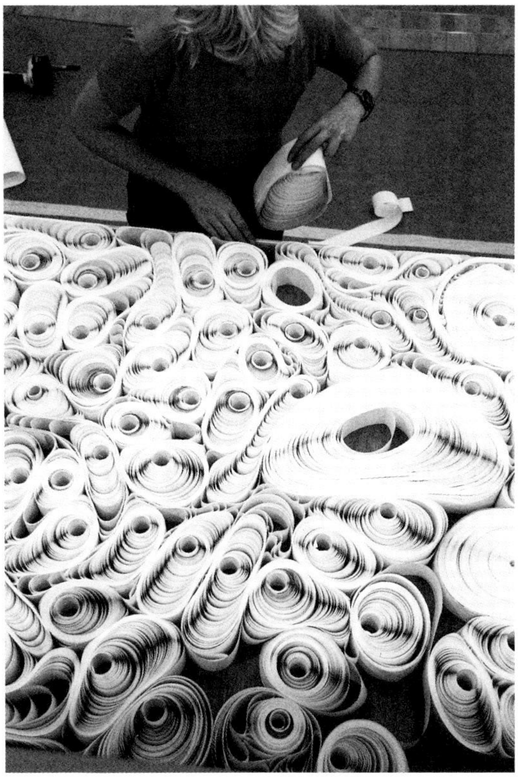

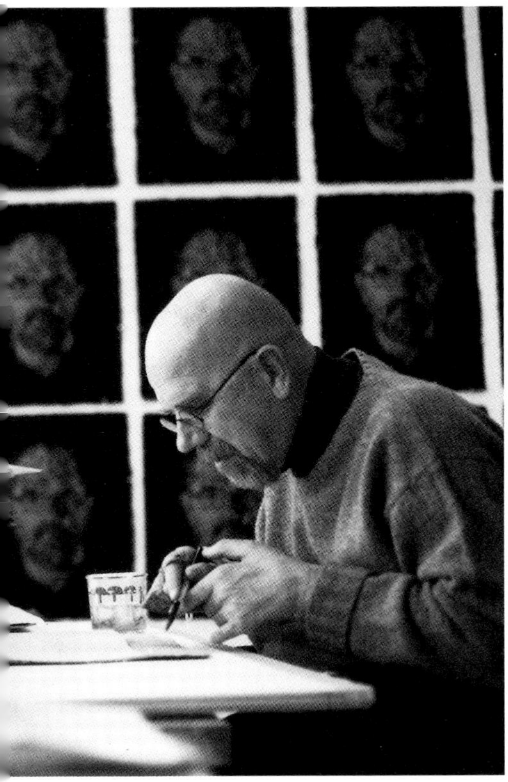

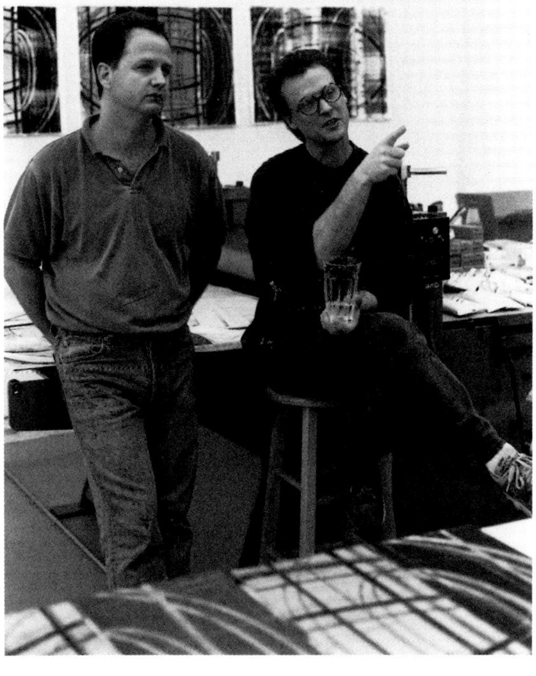

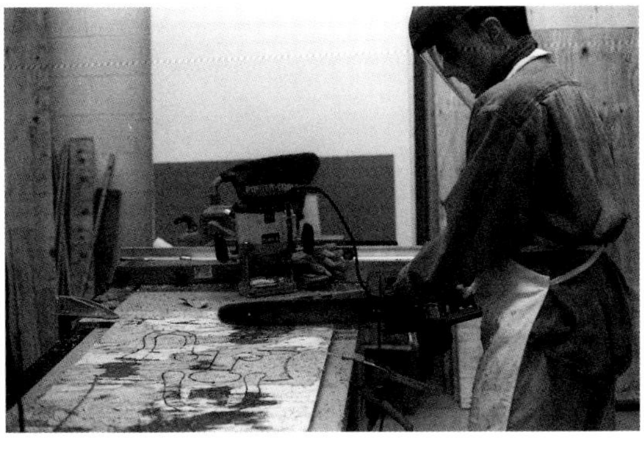

Reflections on Some Prints from Two Palms Press

by Barry Schwabsky

I

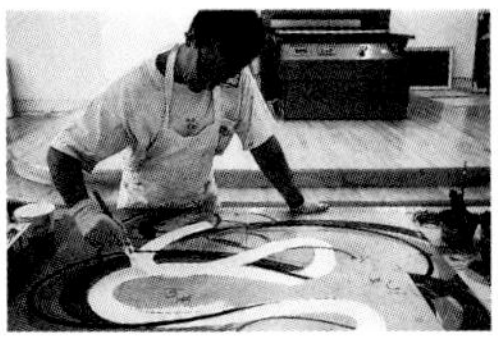

David Row

It's never a bad idea to start where you left off. The lesson comes, again, for instance, from the sequences of monotypes David Row has produced with Two Palms—unique printed images each of which, if you look at them in the order they were done, reveals the ghosts of the ones made before, pale traces woven into the background of the image—which is destined, in turn, to become part of the atmosphere of the next: Row does not wipe the plate clean after he prints each monotype, but rather uses the excess color remaining there (what might be called the material memory of the print he's just made) as the foundation for the next work in the sequence.

I too can refuse to wipe the slate clean, which means that I should start from where I left off when I last had occasion to write—tangentially, that time—about the production of David Lasry's Two Palms Press. What I observed then was that the underlying artistic project animating the enterprise seemed to have something "to do with fathoming the myriad ways that information can be translated into material form, materials imprinted with the trace of an idea." [1] Information: one of the key metaphors of the era of conceptual art (and for that reason the title of an important early exhibition of that art). The word's logic of least resistance leads toward a kind of philosophical idealism, encapsulated in turn by the misleading notion of "dematerialization." But a dialectic between information and materials becomes something else again. Based on an irreducible dualism as it is, such a notion always leads toward the irresolvable: towards tension, paradox, interference, contamination, and irony.

II

Thinking about prints always means thinking about collaboration. Oddly enough, in looking at the prints a particular artist has produced in the course of her career, the emphasis might be less on the individuality of the artist as it has manifested itself in diverse situations than on the differences among the various printers as they have affected the artist's ways of working. Likewise, an exhibition of prints from a single press may be just as likely to showcase the personalities of the various artists who have worked there as to bring out what is specific to the printer. In any situation the variable is likely to draw more attention than the constant. But of course, in any true collaboration there is no constant—each partner is being affected by the other.

Nowhere is that truer than at Two Palms Press. In the five years since David Lasry founded it, Two Palms has collaborated with a fairly limited number of artists, but usually in an intensive fashion. That alone would undoubtedly make for a situation in which artist and printer influence each other deeply. But perhaps more important is the fact that Lasry himself is an artist. His choices of collaborators reflect his artistic interests, not only his technical and economic ones. It's a taste that emphasizes intellect over pathos, deliberation over impulse, structure over sign. The choice also reflects, in part, the network of personal contacts that play an enormous part in forming anyone's artistic outlook; for instance, the artists with whom he's chosen to work include one of his former teachers at the Yale School of Art (Mel Bochner) as well as one of his former Two Palms employees (Pedro Barbeito). Whether the artist is a respected elder or up and coming, the printer's role is to get inside the artists' skin, elicit potentialities the artist may not have realized were there. In that sense, the relation of printer to artist might be compared to that of translator to writer. A literal translation is a literal impossibility. What the translator translates is not the writer's words; it's not even the text, in the narrow sense of that word. What's translated, in the best cases, is the rhythm of the writer's thought on the one hand, his culture, his ethos, on the other. An anecdote Lasry told me

to illustrate how resourceful he'd had to be when getting Two Palms going makes my point: in order to get the attention of Chuck Close, who had been ignoring his requests to consider collaborating, Lasry made up his own print based on one of Close's paintings, sending it to the artist with a note that said, in essence, "Here is what I can do for you." The artist was on the phone the next day; the ruse had worked. Presumptuous? Absolutely. But the bet paid off. Lasry's subliminal message had less to do with technical prowess than with an understanding of what is essential to the art itself.
The message was really: I CAN GET INSIDE YOUR HEAD, BE YOUR HANDS . . . And the record shows that he was right.

III

"All ideas need not be made physical," Sol LeWitt once wrote. [2] But when it does materialize, the idea is inevitably transformed. The material too. They are neither reducible one to the other nor entirely opposed; they are collaborators. LeWitt and Mel Bochner, among the artists who have worked with Two Palms Press, first became known as part of the pioneering generation of conceptual artists in the late 1960s. In both cases, their work has developed in ways that could never have been predicted based on the humble austerities for which it first became known—for LeWitt, skeletal constructions and penciled wall drawings based on numerical permutations; in Bochner's case, arrays of pebbles on the floor and measurements drawn on walls, for instance.

As LeWitt's relief prints here show, he is still working with numerical series, using them in ways that are no longer plain or modest but almost wildly decorative. Where his earlier work could feel willfully blank or even irritating, now it often seeks a sumptuous plenitude. The grid of 36 FIVE-POINTED STARS, 1996, is part of a set of seven such grids representing varieties of stars ranging from three-pointed to nine-pointed (though, frankly, this critic's eye sees the three-pointed "stars" as arrows). All the grids present their repeated image in every possible two-part combination of white, black, and gray and the primary colors red, yellow, and blue. What counts here is not so much the exhaustion of the combinatorial possibilities as what that systematic effort made possible: the liberation of the complete sensorial potential those combinations afford, including the ones that might not gratify the personal taste of the artist (or anyone else in particular).

It also enables the complete separation of the decision-making and executive function in art making, which has always been characteristic of LeWitt. His hands-off approach to his work's execution is exceptional in the Two Palms context: He simply sent the instructions for the prints and left it up to Lasry and his colleagues to decide how to realize them. Indeed, just as LeWitt's wall drawings can be redone from his written instructions (like musical scores) by different people at different times and places—and will always vary accordingly—it is interesting to imagine LeWitt's instructions for these star prints being reinterpreted by various print studios: every version would be different, and assuredly none would have the physical presence of those produced by Two Palms.

Inspired in part, early in his career, by LeWitt, Bochner too works systematically. His prints shown here reflect the "quartet" format he often used in his paintings from the late 1980s to the mid-1990s. They are part of an abstract investigation of perspectival space, and the essential tension that animates them is the one between the "literal" square formed by the juxtaposition of four rectangular sheets (or, in the paintings, canvases) and the squares depicted in perspectival space either in the receding grids that form the underlying ground for each sheet's imagery or in the tumbling cube forms that occupy these spaces. Ironically, the square that is literally there does not exist, except as an absence, and to the extent that our attention is fixed on the depicted perspectival space, we do not actually see this square at all. They are like the duck and rabbit in the famous drawing cited by Wittgenstein: We can see them in alternation, but not simultaneously. On the other hand we can see the depicted shapes as squares only to the extent that we neglect to see that, in fact, they are not squares at all. The simple act of measurement (a recurrent subject in Bochner's art) will show that there are no right angles here at all: except in special cases which do not occur in

Bochner's work, a square in perspectival space is not depicted by a square. Very early in his career, Bochner noticed how perspective "demonstrates not how things appear but rather the working of its own strict postulates." [3] All this might be said to demonstrate the contrary to Frank Stella's famous dictum that "what you see is what you see." [4] In art, Bochner shows, what you see is rarely what you see. But the tension between the two senses of seeing implied in the phrase has never been as strong as in these prints, thanks to Bochner's use of heavy embossment to exaggerate the physical assertiveness of those "illusionistic" cubes.

Close, on the other hand, was not part of conceptual art, but his work was profoundly influenced by it. It, too, has to do with systems—with arrangements of information. But Close did something with information that the conceptualists never considered: He turned it back into pictures. Of course, the clues to why it would be interesting to do such a thing were already lurking in the culture. Just think of the way Roy Lichtenstein—an artist whose profound yet tacit influence on conceptual art has yet to be explored, and whose portrait was painted more than once by Chuck Close—used a simulacrum of newspaper printers' Ben-Day dot pattern to "analyze" his imagery into an underlying system. Close, too, constructs his portraits out of elements that have no representational value in themselves. It is only their relation to the system that lets them produce their illusions. The picture can seem to construct itself and then dissolve before our very eyes, becoming a sequence of arbitrary marks. In the pair of self-portraits shown here, Close pushes this effect even further: the images appear to be almost identical, but subtly each one turns the other inside out: In one, the "positive" elements are printed in black on a white ground while in the other, we see the "negative" spaces around the abstract forms printed in white on a black ground. The artist's face stares out at us as though daring us to try and see through the illusion he weaves and unweaves.

IV

I've given particular attention to the work of LeWitt, Bochner, and Close because, as the oldest and best-established artists in this group, they've left a strong mark on the entire project. Perhaps that becomes clearer when their work is compared to that of the youngest artists in the show, Tara Donovan and Pedro Barbeito. Curious and paradoxical relations between information or systems and materials inform their work too, but in different and perhaps more tacit ways. In Donovan's case, the imagery used in her untitled monotypes may simply seem to be an elegant variant on a familiar form of biomorphic abstraction, sometimes subordinated to a kind of all-over composition (though not entirely, since the edges of the composition are given more emphasis than its center). But you don't need to inspect the works very closely to realize that these snaky or globular forms whose contours contain within themselves innumerable fine lines have not been drawn by any normal method. Surely one would go mad trying to execute such things by hand. In fact, the images were "drawn" by assembling rolls of unspooled adding machine paper and then inking their edges. On one level, Donovan's monotypes might seem to be entirely about materials. Certainly they feature an entirely original way of using a material that has hardly ever been used in art otherwise. But it's far from a raw material. It's something that has been produced and formed precisely with the idea of information in mind—what is an adding machine, after all, but a simple information processing device? While Donovan's work may appear to emphasize materials (yet turns out to reflect on information as well), Barbeito's, contrariwise, seems dominated by information, for which the work's material aspect is merely a secondary presentational necessity; likewise, appearances are deceiving. Investigations into the PHYSICS & TECHNOLOGY OF QUANTUM-CONFINED MOLECULAR & ELECTRONIC DEVICES—the title of a recent painting, from a series directly related to the prints Barbeito made with Two Palms—gives the flavor of his subject matter: information gathered from astronomical research translated into visual form. But a strange confounding of the categories happens as a result. The positive-negative dualism of digital information—that endless series of ones and zeros—not only reveals itself as an essential material difference (here, the distinction between white and black) but moreover as essentially a series of imprints upon an underlying material (in this case, paper).

V

Perhaps, then, the relation information/material corresponds to the relation digital/analog, but the important thing to keep in mind is the way art (and not only art) keeps reminding us that nothing is ever simply digital or analog, information or material, all the way through. What is analog at one level turns out to be digital at another and vice-versa. Information is an underlying condition of matter, matter the ground of information. That's a realization that comes just as easily from Terry Winters' series GRAPHIC PRIMITIVES, 1998, as it does from Barbeito's work. Along with Row, Carroll Dunham, and Jessica Stockholder, Winters represents what might be called a middle generation among the artists who've worked at Two Palms Press. His prints were the result of a series of what might be called translations and retranslations between analog and digital modes: Winters redrew some existing drawings on a computer so that the images could be laser-cut into woodblocks. These were then printed in white oil paint on white Japanese paper; finally a wash of black ink soaked into the paper but not into the paint, on which it left but a shadow of gray, thereby revealing the image by darkening the ground on which it appears. What's important is not how the images came into being, though, so much as the way the art that results from that mixture of processes somehow cut across some of the categories by which we normally read images: They simultaneously recall electronic circuitry, urban cartographies, and diagrams of biological systems. The way they look reflects the interchange between culture, technology, and the individual that brought them into being. No wonder John Rajchman was moved to speak of "the electronic brain-city" when writing about them. [5]

Dunham, Stockholder, and Row each play his or her own variations on our theme of information and materials. Such concerns may seem furthest from Dunham—an imagist in a way that none of these other artists is, even Close. His figures of cartoon-like violence may seem like straightforward icons of a savage culture—but look at the way he calls attention to the plywood matrix from which his image has been printed: It's as though the material itself were giving rise to this comically nightmarish semblance, as though matter itself were, like Goya's "sleep of reason," giving birth to monsters. Stockholder's fascination with materials is more obvious; she is a great observer of the innate capacities of ordinary stuff. But the systematic nature of her use of them—the calculation underlying her whimsy—only emerges with prolonged consideration. The succession of materials and matrixes in each one is basically a sequence of simple positives and negatives (those digital ones and zeros again), but the results of the interactions and interferences among those sequences is complex. Row may be as straightforwardly an abstractionist as Dunham is an imagist, which is to say, not at all: Such straightforwardness turns out to have unexpected layers to it. The looping lines of his recent work certainly refer to the free-hand gestures of Abstract Expressionism but, made with stencils, they are not unique but rather endlessly replicable. In his monotypes, Row gives this replicability an added dimension. A monotype is typically a one-shot action, an indirect or reversed form of painting that exhausts itself in a single imprint, but in Row's, each haunted by the last, the knot of time and space seems to have become strangely loosened, a texture unraveled. Perhaps the dichotomy of information and matter reduces to this: Information is the form of memory, matter the trace of what is remembered.

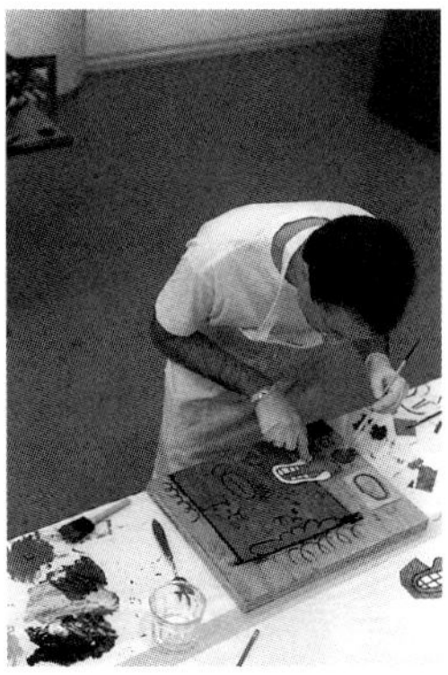

Carroll Dunham

1. "The Weight of Thought," DAVID LASRY: DRAWINGS, PRINTS, COLLABORATIONS (New York: Wynn Kramarsky, 1998).
2. LeWitt, "Sentences on Conceptual Art" (1969), in CONCEPTUAL ART: A CRITICAL ANTHOLOGY, ed. by Alexander Alberro and Blake Stimson (Cambridge: MIT Press, 1999), p. 107.
3. Bochner, "The Serial Attitude" (1967), in CONCEPTUAL ART, ed. by Alberro and Stimson, p. 26.
4. Dan Flavin, Donald Judd, and Frank Stella, "New Nihilism or New Art? Interview with Bruce Glaser" (1964) in MINIMALISM, ed. by James Meyer (London: Phaidon Press, 2000), p. 199.
5. John Rajchman, "Painting in the Brain-City," TERRY WINTERS: GRAPHIC PRIMITIVES (New York: Matthew Marks Gallery, 1999), p. 15.

1 SAMPEX 2000
Relief print with embossment, collaged engraving and applied archival ink-jet print on handmade paper
15 x 21 inches

2 ROSAT 2000
Relief print with embossment, collaged engraving and applied archival ink-jet print on handmade paper
15 x 21 inches

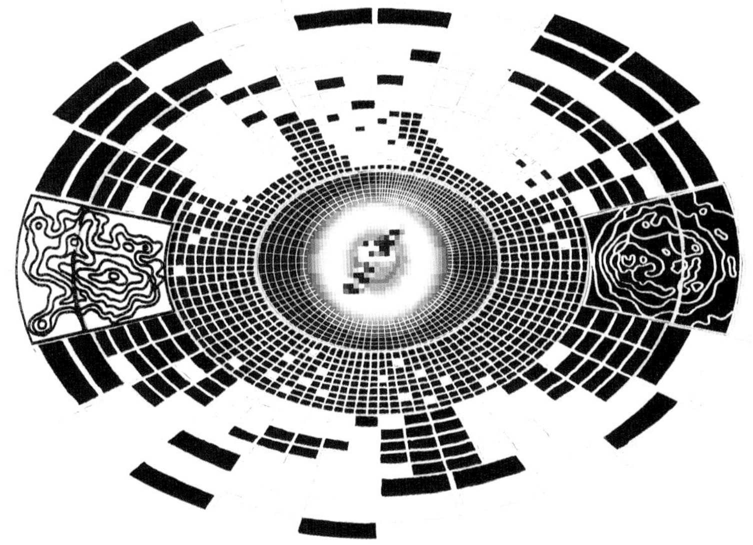

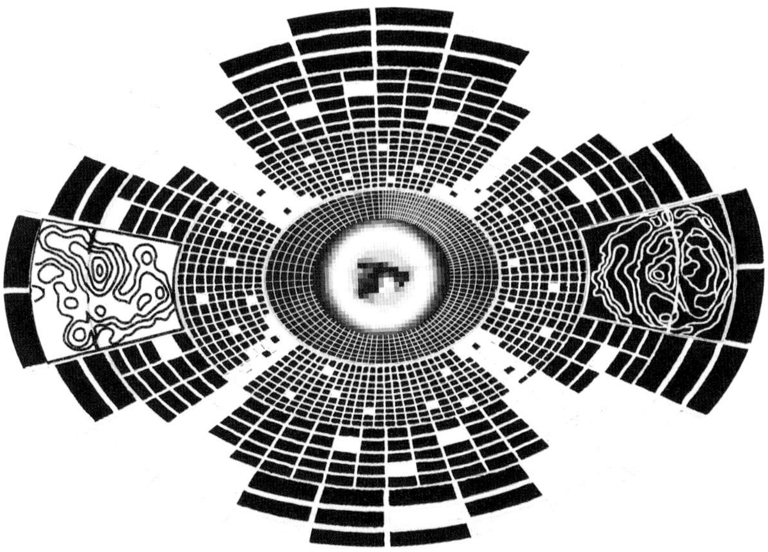

3 NOT TITLED 1995
Monotype on handmade paper
18 x 36 inches

4 GENETIC SPACE (BLACK & WHITE 2) 1996
Engraving on handmade paper
36 x 36 inches
Edition of 6

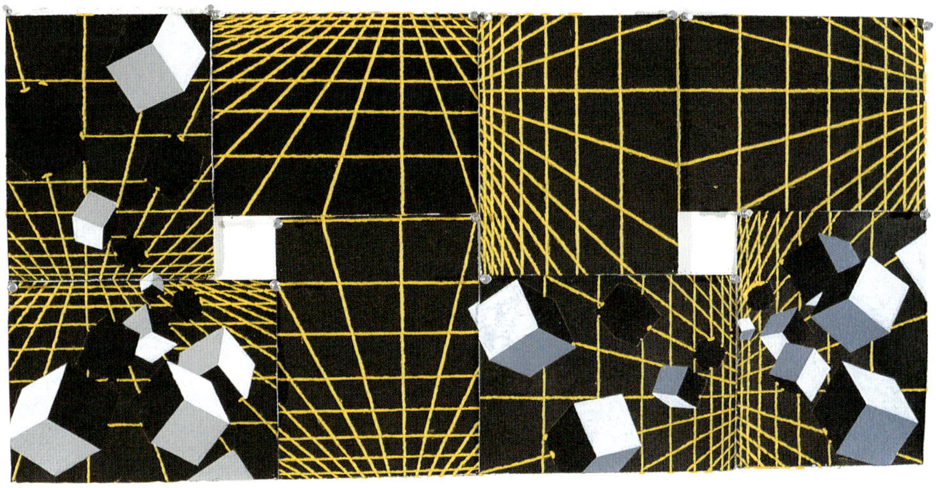

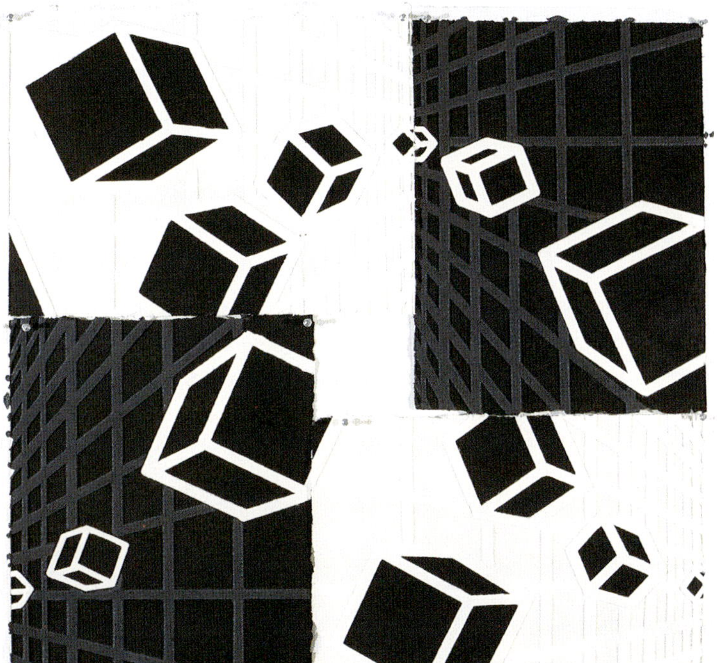

5 SELF-PORTRAIT 1 1999
Relief print with embossment on blue/gray Twinrocker handmade paper
25 x 20 inches
Edition of 50

6 SELF-PORTRAIT 2 1999
Relief print with embossment on black Twinrocker handmade paper
25 x 20 inches
Edition of 50

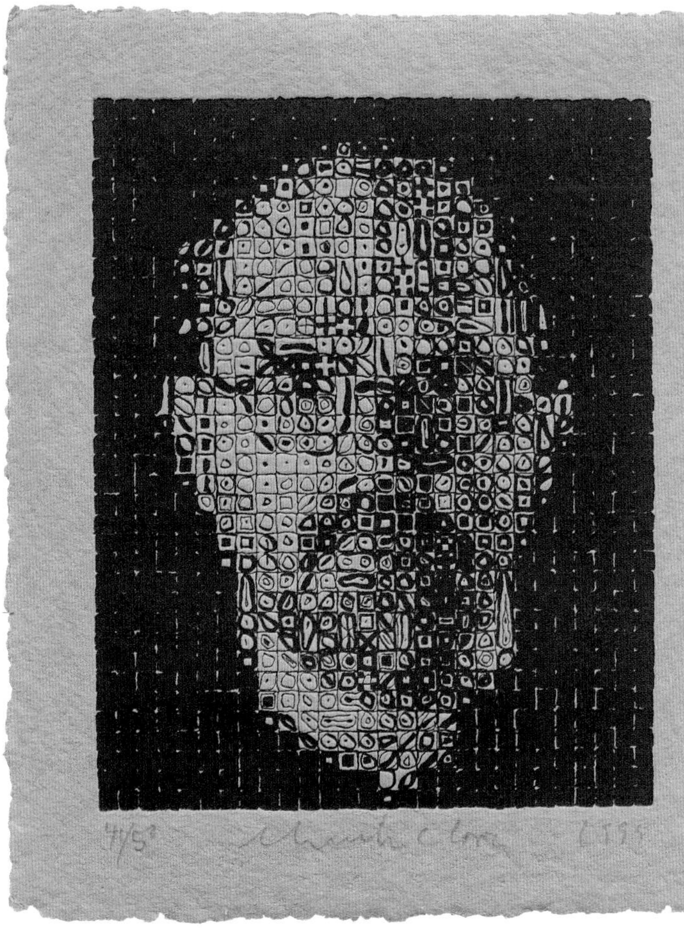

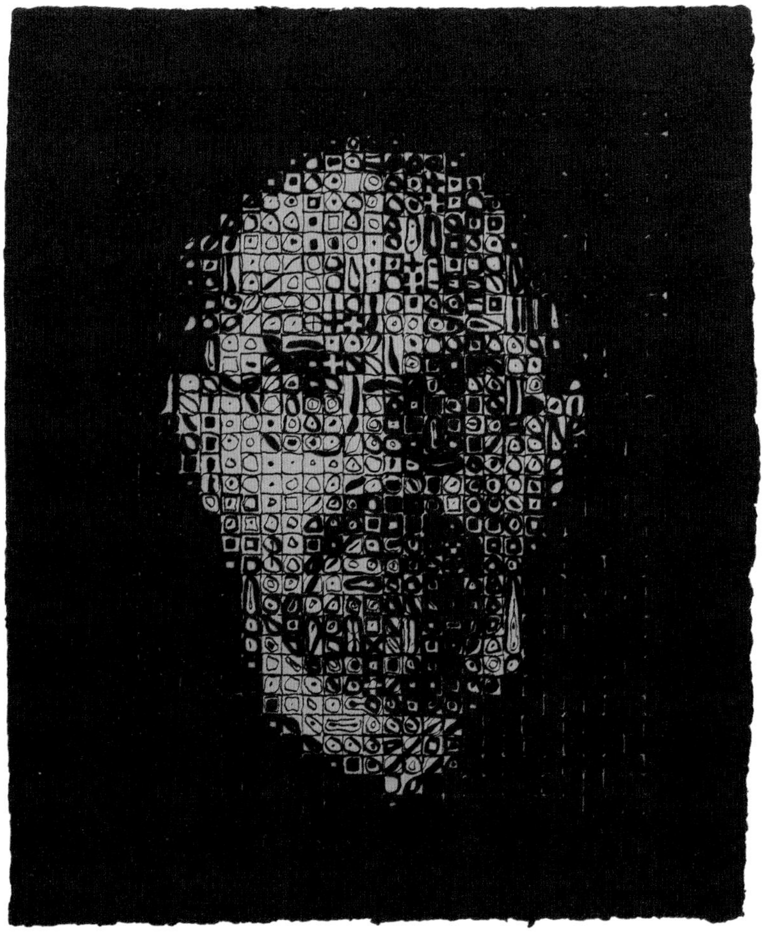

7 UNTITLED 2000
Monotype on Twinrocker handmade paper
47 x 34 inches

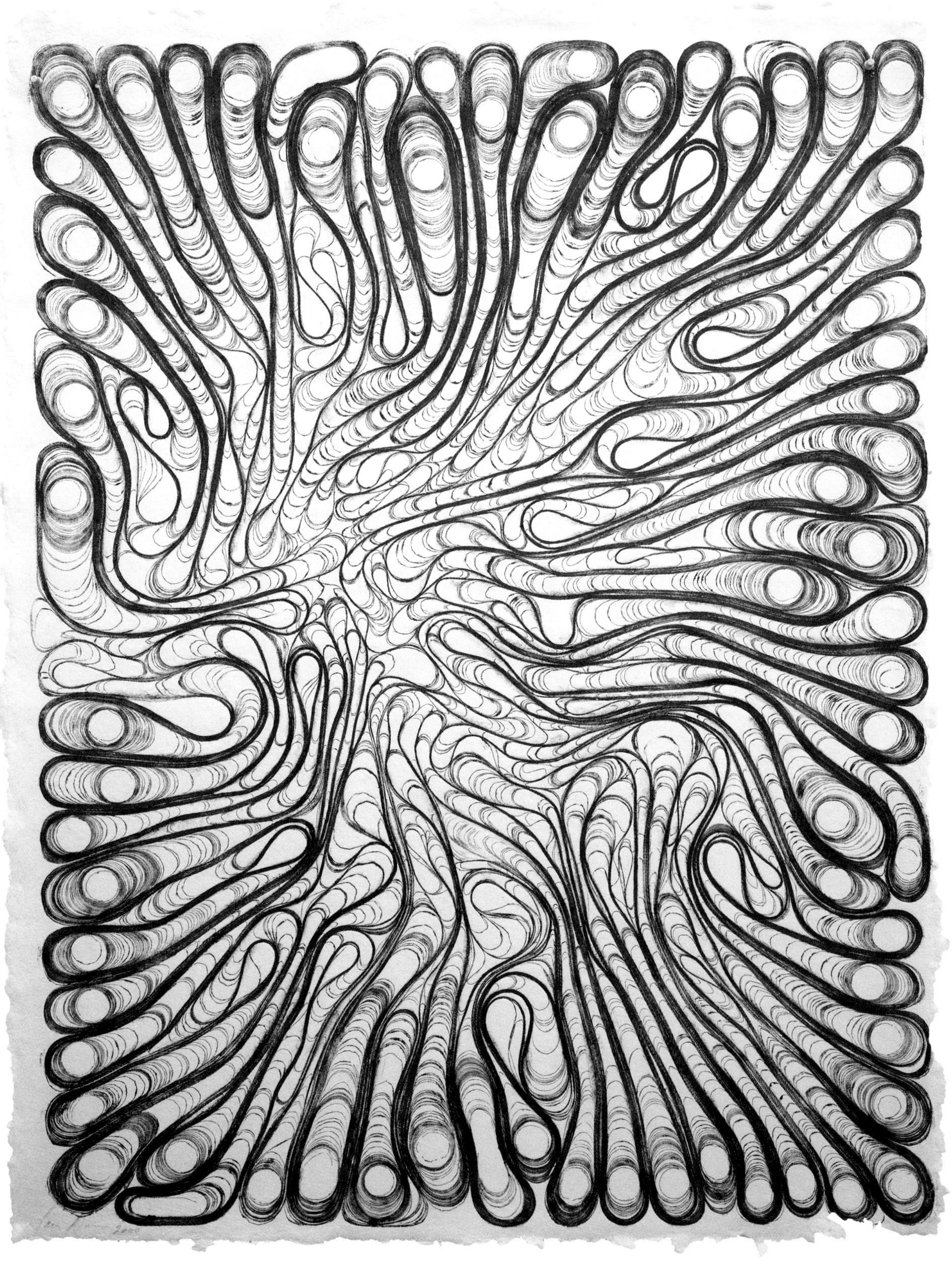

8 KILLER 2000
Wood engraving with embossment on handmade paper
34 x 47 inches
Edition of 12

9 UNTITLED 2000
Wood engraving with embossment on handmade paper
22 x 29 inches
Edition of 12

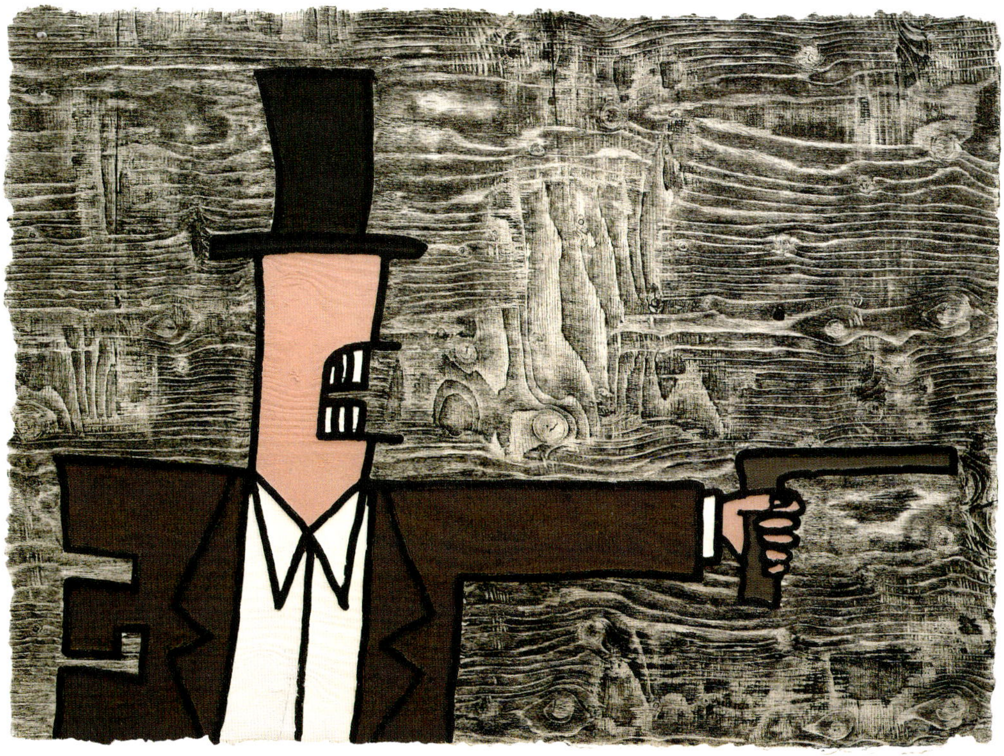

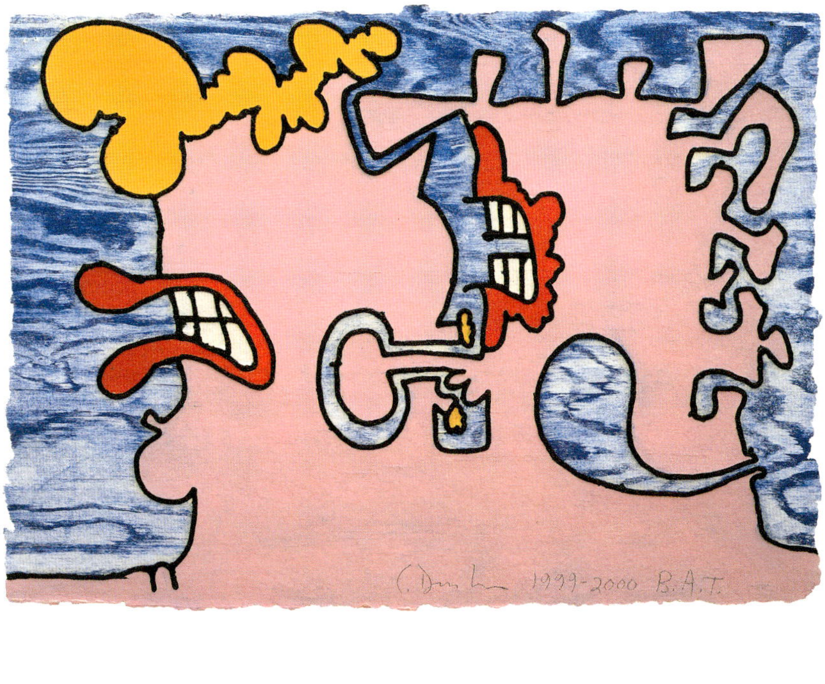
1999-2000 B.A.T.

10 FIVE-POINTED STARS 1996
Relief print on tinted handmade paper
36 individually printed stars
54 x 54 inches overall
Edition of 15

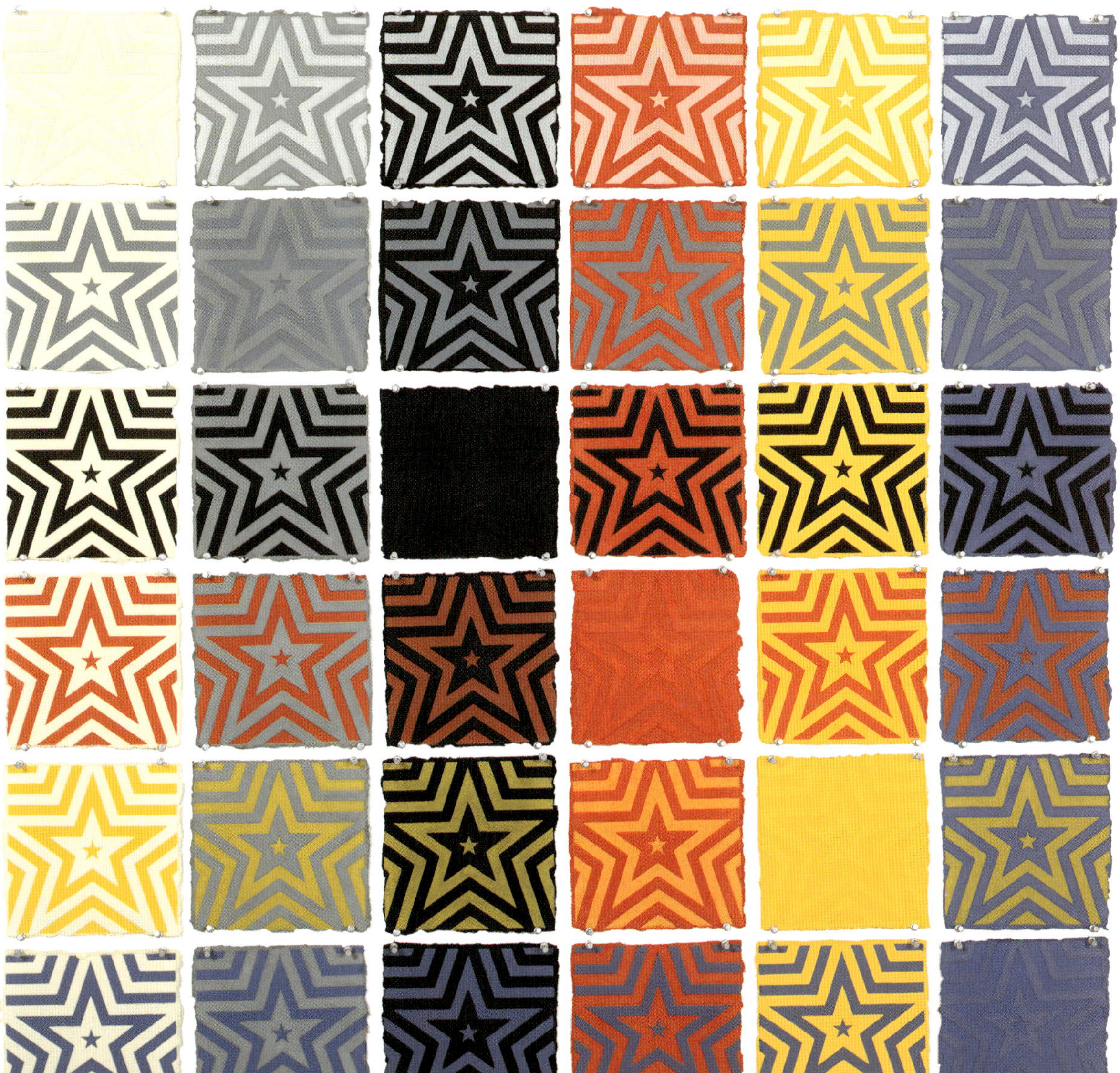

11 UNTITLED 2000
Monotype on handmade paper
34 x 47 inches

12 UNTITLED 2000
Monotype on handmade paper
34 x 47 inches

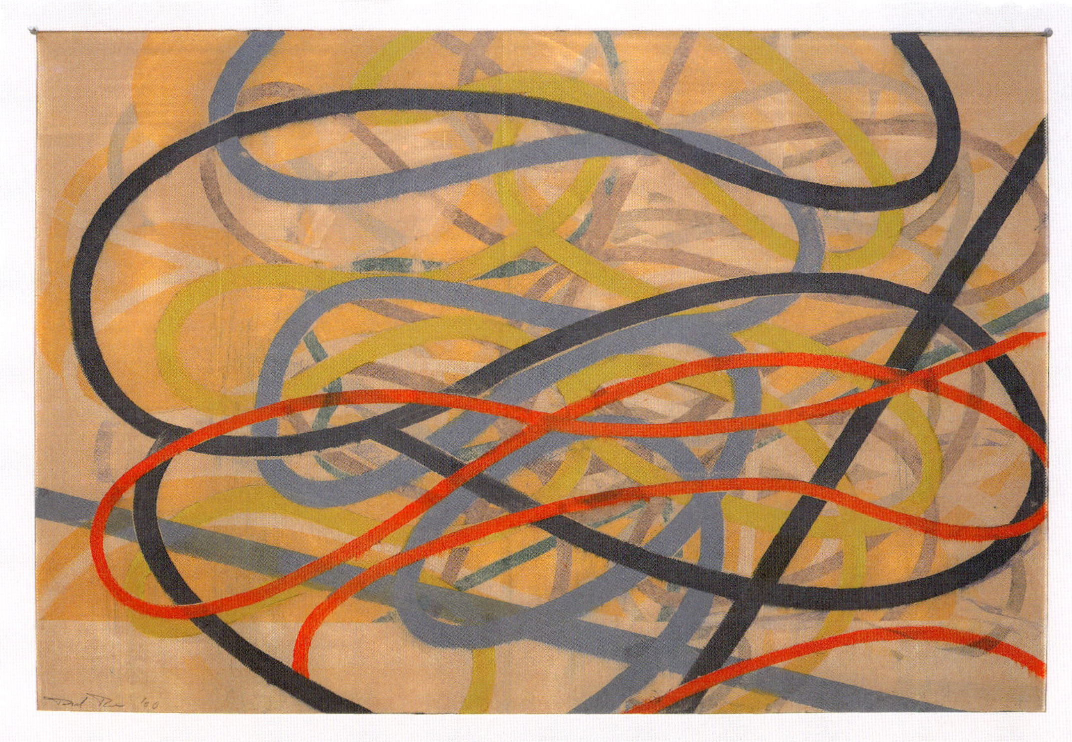

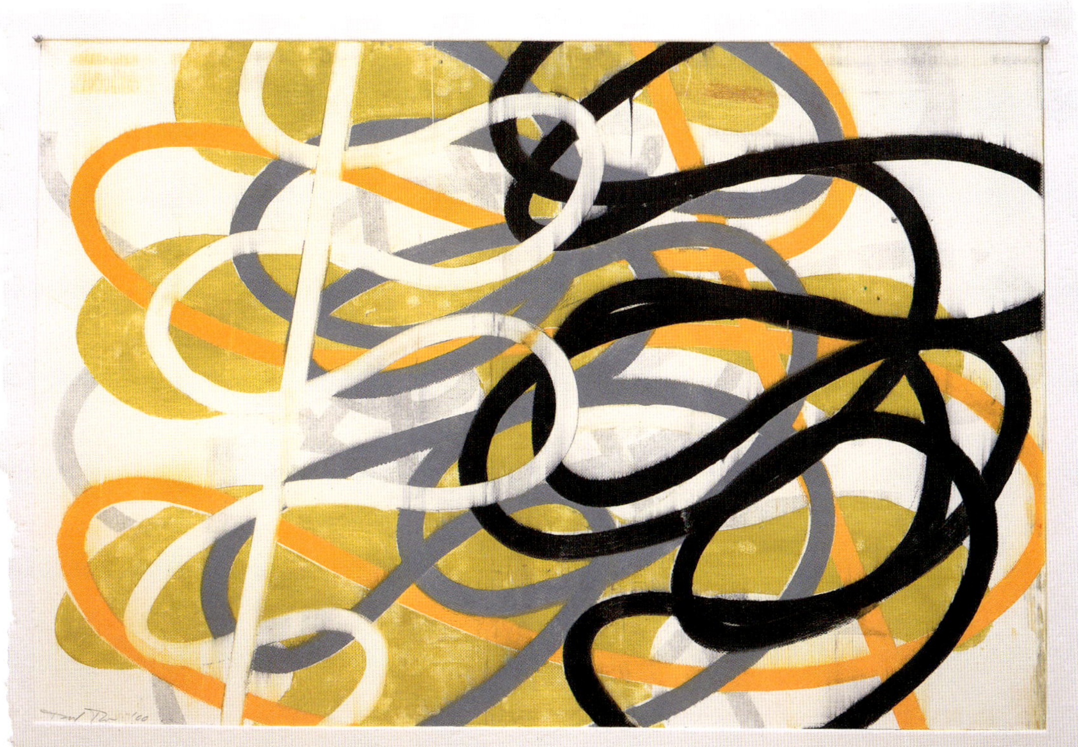

JESSICA STOCKHOLDER

13 UNTITLED 2000
Monotype with wood engraving, linoleum, orange upholstery
and fake fur on Twinrocker handmade paper
34 x 46 inches

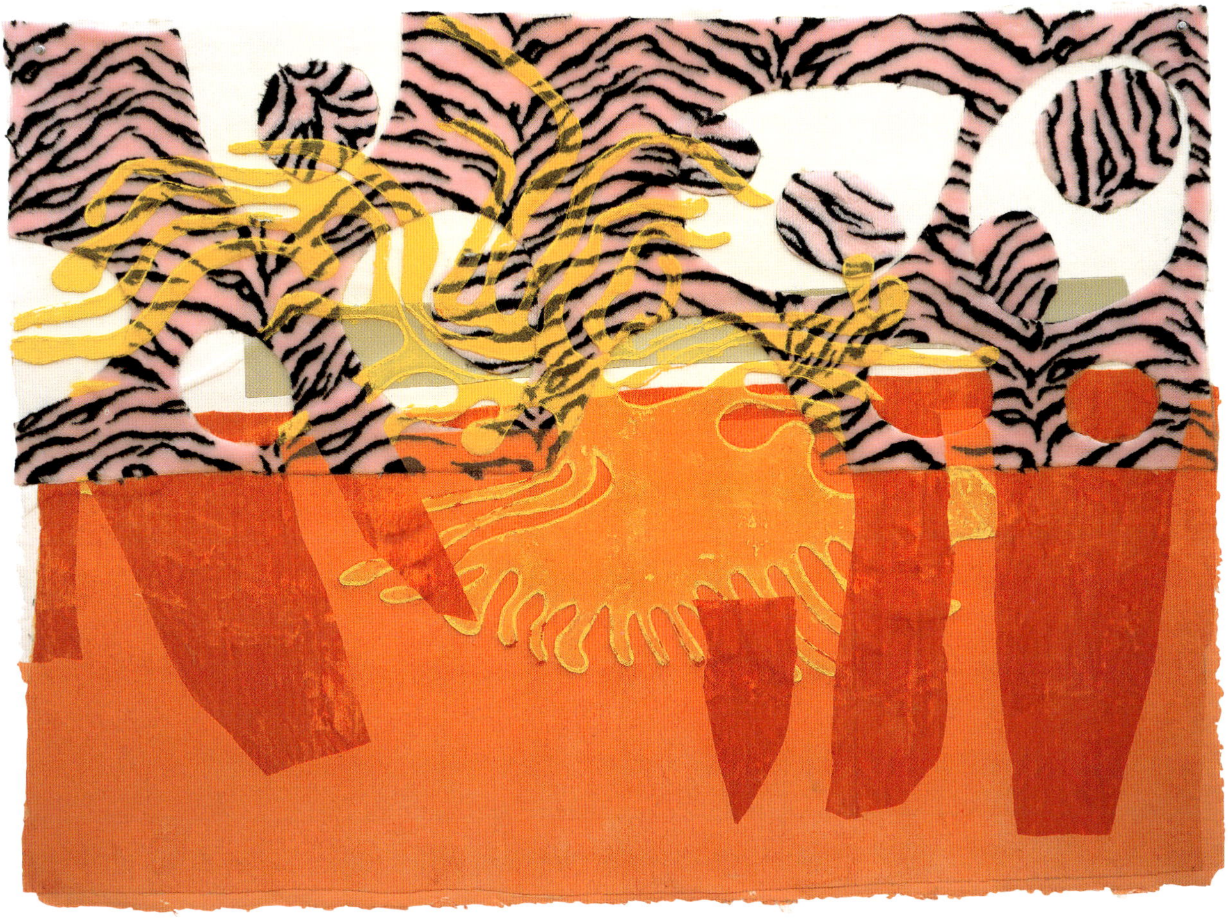

14 GRAPHIC PRIMITIVES 1998
Portfolio of 9 rinsed woodcuts on Japanese Kochi paper
20 1/4 x 26 inches each
Edition of 35

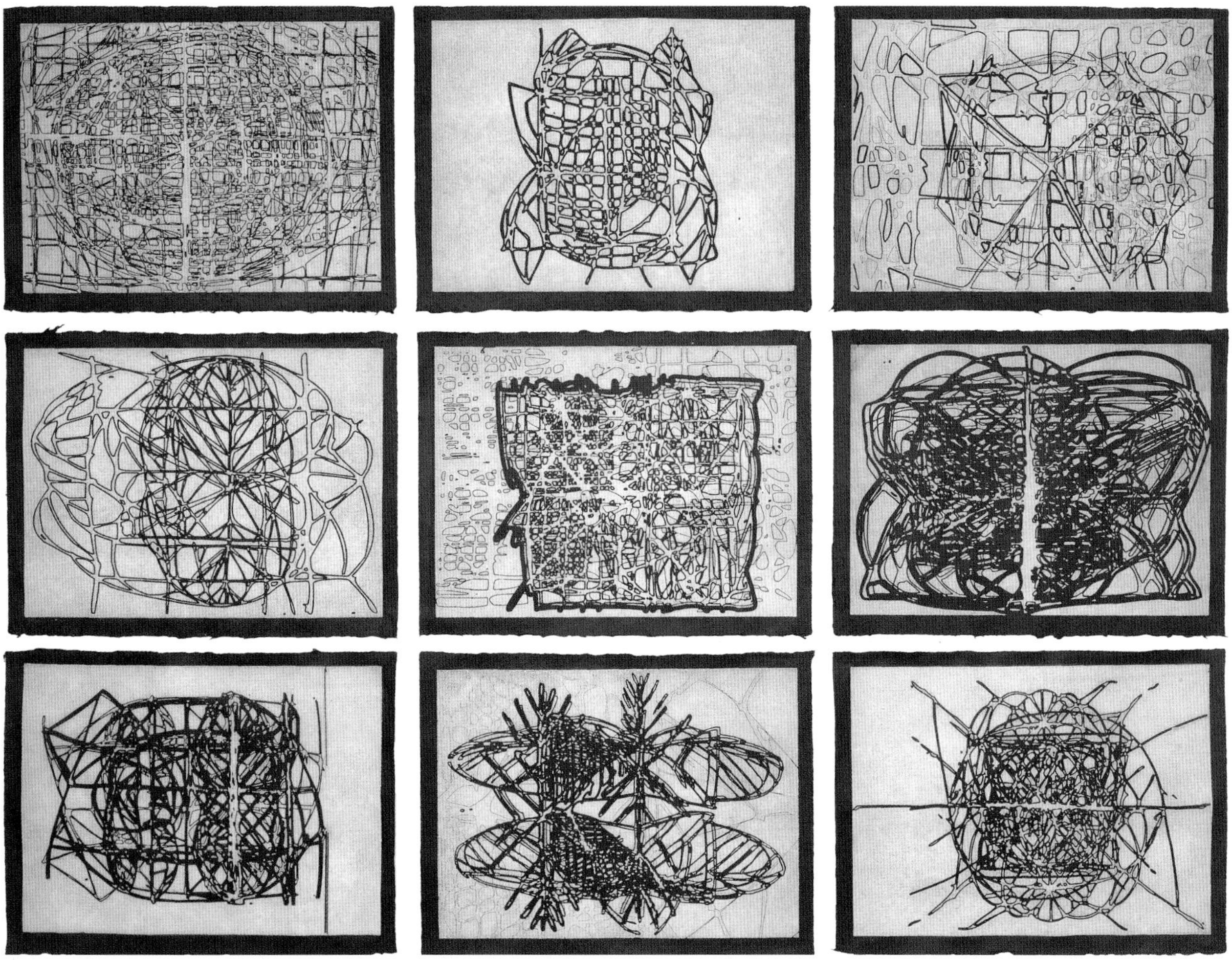

Unless indicated otherwise, all works are in the collection of
Two Palms Press

Pedro Barbeito
SAMPEX 2000
Relief print with embossment, collaged engraving and applied archival ink-jet print on handmade paper
15 x 21 inches

Pedro Barbeito
ROSAT 2000
Relief print with embossment, collaged engraving and applied archival ink-jet print on handmade paper
15 x 21 inches

Pedro Barbeito
CHANDRA 2 2000
Relief print with embossment, collaged engraving and applied archival ink-jet print on black-dyed handmade paper
15 x 21 inches

Pedro Barbeito
CGRO 2 2000
Relief print with embossment, collaged engraving and applied archival ink-jet print on black-dyed handmade paper
15 x 21 inches

Mel Bochner
NOT TITLED 1995
Monotype on handmade paper
18 x 36 inches

Mel Bochner
GENETIC SPACE (BLACK & WHITE 2) 1996
Engraving on handmade paper
36 x 36 inches
Edition of 6

Mel Bochner
UNTITLED 2000
Monotype on handmade paper
34 x 47 inches

Chuck Close
SELF-PORTRAIT 1 1999
Relief print with embossment on blue/gray Twinrocker handmade paper
25 x 20 inches
Edition of 50

Chuck Close
SELF-PORTRAIT 2 1999
Relief print with embossment on black Twinrocker handmade paper
25 x 20 inches
Edition of 50

Tara Donovan
UNTITLED 2000
Monotype on Twinrocker handmade paper
47 x 34 inches

Tara Donovan
UNTITLED 2000
3 monotypes on Twinrocker handmade paper
30 x 22 inches each

Carroll Dunham
KILLER 2000
Wood engraving with embossment on handmade paper
34 x 47 inches
Edition of 12

Carroll Dunham
UNTITLED 2000
Wood engraving on handmade paper
22 x 29 inches
Edition of 12

Carroll Dunham
WAITING FOR WOOD 1995–96
7 monotypes on handmade paper
14 x 18 inches each

Sol LeWitt
FIVE-POINTED STARS 1996
Relief print on tinted handmade paper
36 individually printed stars
54 x 54 inches overall
Edition of 15

Sol LeWitt
EIGHT-POINTED STARS 1996
Relief print on tinted handmade paper
36 individually printed stars
54 x 54 inches overall
Edition of 15

David Row
UNTITLED 1995
Monotype on handmade paper
22 x 30 inches

David Row
UNTITLED 2000
Monotype on handmade paper
34 x 47 inches

David Row
UNTITLED 2000
Monotype on handmade paper
34 x 47 inches
Collection David Row

Jessica Stockholder
TURNING PAPER 1998
Monotype with wood engraving, embossment, shag carpet and orange peels on Twinrocker handmade paper
22 x 30 inches

Jessica Stockholder
TURNING PAPER 1998
Monotype with wood engraving, embossment and wool sweater on Twinrocker handmade paper
22 x 30 inches

Jessica Stockholder
UNTITLED 2000
Monotype with wood engraving, linoleum, orange upholstery and fake fur on Twinrocker handmade paper
34 x 46 inches

Terry Winters
GRAPHIC PRIMITIVES 1998
Portfolio of 9 rinsed woodcuts on Japanese Kochi paper
20 1/4 x 26 inches each
Edition of 35

1979–83	Attends University of California, Davis where he studies with Wayne Thiebaud; graduates with a BA in Studio Art and Political Science.
1983–85	Enters and completes the MFA program at the Yale University School of Art where he studies with William Bailey, Mel Bochner, Jake Berthot, and Bernard Chaet.
1988–90	Head printer at the Garner Tullis Workshop in New York City; works with artists Sam Francis, Helen Frankenthaler, Sean Scully, John Walker, and other artists making monotypes and woodblock prints using an industrial hydraulic press.
1991–94	Focuses on his own artwork; exhibits paintings, prints, and drawings in Basel, Chicago, New York, Paris, San Diego, San Francisco, and Tokyo.
1993	Receives Visual Arts Fellowship, National Endowment for the Arts.
1994	Starts and operates Two Palms Press. Invites David Row to the press (the first collaboration). Mel Bochner begins an ongoing print project later that year.
1995	Carroll Dunham, Sol LeWitt, Jacqueline Humphries, and Nancy Haynes initiate and complete projects that result in innovative techniques to meet their needs and ideas.
1996	Starts dialogue with Terry Winters who comes to the press the following year.
1997	Develops prototype print for Chuck Close as a means of enticing the artist to start a project with the press. Close subsequently begins Self-Portrait series.

1998 Jessica Stockholder accepts invitation to work. Her project presents new challenges as she intends to use everyday objects as printing material.

1999 Explores 3-D printing with Kiki Smith using stereo lithography. The project is unsuccessful and evolves instead into a bronze multiple. Initiates second project with Chuck Close.

2000 Tara Donovan and Pedro Barbeito further test the press's commitment to innovation. Donovan's plates are made of spooled paper; Barbeito's 3-tiered plates, from acrylic dyes. Carroll Dunham returns to the press for a second project.